KNOCKOUT!

KNOCKOUT!

A PHOTOBIOGRAPHY OF BOXER

JOE LOUIS

BY GEORGE SULLIVAN

NATIONAL GEOGRAPHIC

WASHINGTON, D.C.

PUBLISHED BY THE NATIONAL GEOGRAPHIC SOCIETY

John M. Fahey, Jr., *President and Chief Executive Officer*

Gilbert M. Grosvenor, *Chairman of the Board*

Tim T. Kelly, *President, Global Media Group*

John Q. Griffin, *President, Publishing*

Nina D. Hoffman, *Executive Vice President; President, Book Publishing Group*

PREPARED BY THE BOOK DIVISION

Nancy Laties Feresten, *Vice President, Editor in Chief, Children's Books*

Bea Jackson, *Director of Design and Illustrations, Children's Books*

Amy Shields, *Executive Editor, Series, Children's Books*

Jennifer Emmett, *Executive Editor, Reference and Solo, Children's Books*

Carl Mehler, *Director of Maps*

STAFF FOR THIS BOOK

Virginia Koeth, *Editor*

Lori Epstein, *Illustrations Editor*

Marty Ittner, *Designer*

Martin Walz, *Map Production*

Lewis Bassford, *Production Project Manager*

Jennifer A. Thornton, *Managing Editor*

Grace Hill, *Associate Managing Editor*

R. Gary Colbert, *Production Director*

Susan Borke, *Legal and Business Affairs*

MANUFACTURING AND QUALITY MANAGEMENT

Christopher A. Liedel, *Chief Financial Officer*

Phillip L. Schlosser, *Vice President*

Chris Brown, *Technical Director*

Nicole Elliott, *Manager*

LIBRARY OF CONGRESS CATALOGING-IN-PUBLICATION DATA

Sullivan, George, 1927-

Knockout! a photobiography of boxer Joe Louis / by George Sullivan. -- 1st ed.

    p. cm.

Includes bibliographical references and index.

ISBN 978-1-4263-0328-9 (hardcover : alk. paper) --
ISBN 978-1-4263-0329-6 (library binding : alk. paper)

1. Louis, Joe, 1914-1981. 2. Boxers (Sports)--United States--Biography. 3. African American boxers--Biography. I. Title.

GV1132.L6S85 2008

796.83092--dc22

[B]

                    2008025036

Printed in the United States of America

TITLE PAGE: With his crushing right hand and powerful jab, Joe Louis was hailed as the hardest-punching heavyweight of all time.

OPPOSITE PAGE: During the years of his greatest success, it was said that more was written about Joe Louis than anyone, with the exception of Charles Lindbergh, the aviator who made the first solo nonstop flight across the Atlantic Ocean.

PHOTO CREDITS

Alabama Dept. of Archives and History: 8 background, 10 bottom; Bettmann/Corbis: Front cover, back cover, 2-3, 5, 10 top, 15, 16-17, 21, 23 inset, 24, 26, 31, 32, 34-35, 38, 41 inset, 42, 44 inset, 45, 48-49, 47 inset, 50, 54 background, 56-57, 60; Corbis: 54 inset, 58; Detroit Public Library, Burton Historical Collection: 8 inset, 13, 28-29, 41 background; Lori Epstein: 63 both; Getty Images: 15 background (Fox Photos/Hulton Archive), 36 (Joseph Scherschel/Time Life Pictures), 47 background (Frank Driggs Collection), 53 (Gjon Mili/Time Life Pictures), 55 (Keystone); www.ha.com: dust jacket: front flap and back cover tickets, 6, 18, 20, 33, 43, 62

The body text is set in New Century Schoolbook.

The display text is set in Goshen and Knockout.

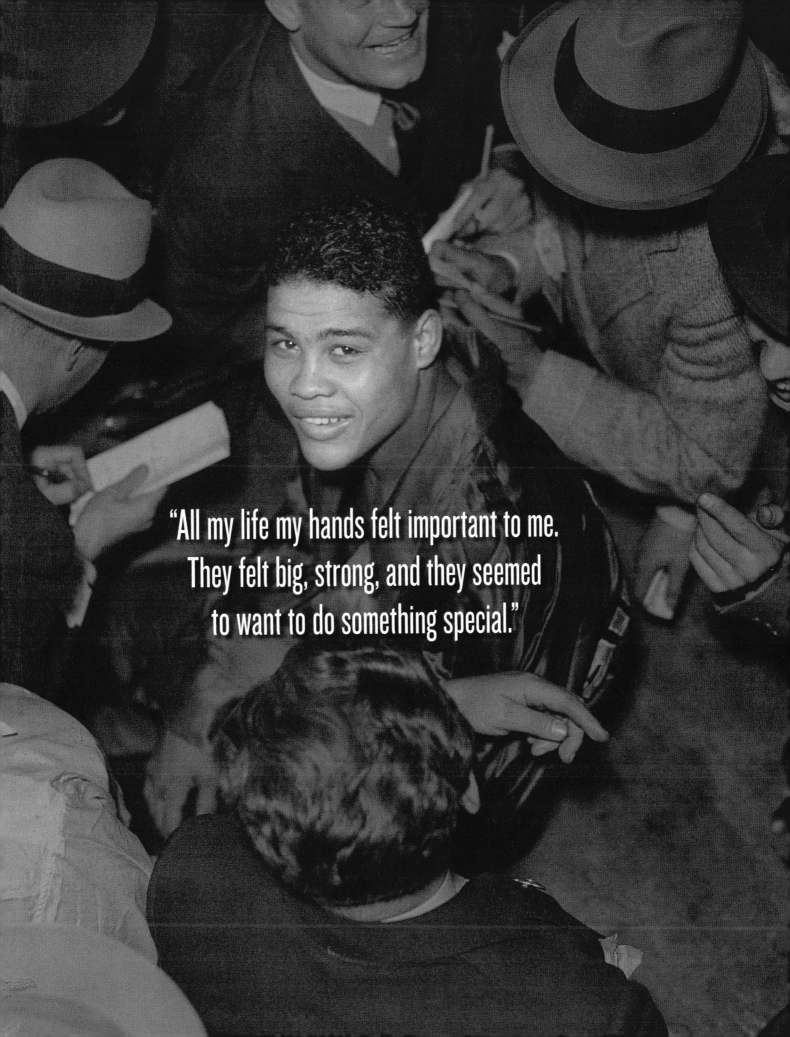

"All my life my hands felt important to me. They felt big, strong, and they seemed to want to do something special."

A poster promoting a newsreel showing of Louis's fight against Billy Conn, held at Yankee Stadium in New York in 1946.

FOREWORD

I grew up on the South Side of Chicago, where my father's name and face appeared on milk cartons and was a household name. Yet, I did not fully appreciate my father, Joe Louis, until I was in high school. I was fortunate to attend private schools because of his financial success. There were times when parents of my classmates, once they realized who my father was, would tell me how important my dad was to them and how significant he was to society overall. Their comments were puzzling at the time.

It would frustrate my sister Jackie and me when our father would take us to dinner at a restaurant and we were constantly interrupted by his many fans, people wanting an autograph or to reflect on special times spent with him in the army, at a certain fight, or mutual gathering. It was our private time, yet we were forced to share our father with the world.

I remember my graduation from the University of Denver. All heads turned when my father entered the arena. Although I could not see his face, I knew it was him. There was a buzz in the room as people stood to get a glimpse of the Champ. It was clear that my father meant a great deal to many people—black, white, Jew, gentile, rich and poor.

A fan once told me that he became a college dean because my father gave him the sense of self-worth and respect that led him to do more than what was expected of him as a young black living in Pittsburgh, working in the steel mills. Joe Louis is truly an American success story—a young black who transcended race and emerged as a hero. He impacted an entire society and challenged a country not only to respect his accomplishments in the ring, but also to examine their own segregated views toward African Americans.

Knockout! is the story of Joe Louis, my father, a man who made a significant difference in how we live today.

Joseph Louis Barrow, Jr.

**W**hen young Joe Louis started his boxing career in the 1930s, America was a different kind of place for black Americans. They suffered as victims of segregation and bigotry that reached into every part of their lives. In magazines, books, movies, and on radio, they often heard themselves described as lazy and stupid. They faced discrimination when seeking jobs or places to live. Many lived in poverty and without hope.

In the South, racial segregation was in force. Most African Americans there worked on farms or in mean and lowly jobs. They could not vote freely. They were barred from "whites only" schools, churches, movie theaters, and restrooms. They could not drink from public water fountains and were made to ride in the backs of buses.

At various times, waves of lynchings swept the South. In 1933 alone, 42 African Americans suffered death by hanging at the hands of angry lynch mobs.

Black athletes are now outstanding figures in American sports. Some, like basketball's Michael Jordan, golf's Tiger Woods, and the Williams sisters in tennis, have become superstars and celebrities. But in the 1930s, black faces were rare in professional sports. Baseball barred blacks. So did pro football. The National Basketball Association, the NBA, didn't begin to accept African Americans until 1950.

Unlike other sports, boxing gave blacks a chance to participate. During Joe Louis's championship years, the sport enjoyed a golden era, with only baseball and college football rivaling it in importance. Despite boxing's enormous popularity, African Americans found that whites ruled the sport, and the path to real success was always difficult and discouraging as a result.

Young Joe Louis (top row, center) with other amateur boxers of the early 1930s.

Background: The countryside of Chambers County in east-central Alabama, where Joe Louis was born.

"Momma was a big woman, my father was a big man. We came from big people, mostly blacks, some whites, and a few powerful Indians; put that all together and I guess you get something."

Joe Louis was able to avoid boxing's pitfalls. He used his skills to win the heavyweight boxing championship in 1937 and to become a true American hero. In a time before Jackie Robinson and Dr. Martin Luther King, Jr., Louis showed that, given a chance, African Americans could excel. Good-natured and dignified outside the ring, Joe Louis came to stand as a symbol of hope and pride to black Americans.

Joe Louis grew up in Detroit and did his first boxing there. He later made his home in Chicago for several years. Still later, he lived in Las Vegas. But Louis always thought of Detroit as his home.

Louis's liking for Detroit began when he was about 12. His family moved north to Detroit from Chambers County, Alabama. There, in a shabby four-room house at the foot of Buckalew Mountain, about six miles from the town of Lafayette,

Top: Joe's mother, Lillian Barrow Brooks, whispers to her son during a break at Louis's Pompton Lakes, New Jersey, training camp in June 1935. Bottom: Monroe Barrow, Louis's father, in a photograph taken at a state mental hospital for African Americans in Mount Vernon, Alabama, in 1938.

Joe was born. The date was May 13, 1914.

Joe was the seventh of eight children of Monroe Barrow, the son of a slave, and his wife Lilly Riece Barrow. Monroe Barrow was a big man, over six feet tall. He weighed 200 pounds.

Joe's father and his family were sharecroppers. They worked to raise cotton on a piece of land that they rented from whites. Sharecroppers also bought seed, fertilizer, tools, farm equipment, and farm animals from the landowner. When they sold their crops, they paid the amount they owed to the landowner. The debt was often so large that the sharecropper and his family could not pay the whole amount. The family ended up working all of their lives to settle it. To many, sharecropping was simply a legal form of slavery.

When Joe was two, his father suffered a breakdown. It might have been the hard work. Or perhaps he had come to realize that the more he worked, the more he owed. He had to be taken away to a mental institution. He later died there.

After the loss of her husband, Louis's mother continued to work the farm. "She worked as hard, and many times harder, than any man around," Joe said. "She could plow a good straight furrow, plant and pick [cotton] with the best of them—cut cord wood like a lumberjack, then leave the fields an hour earlier than anyone else and fix a meal to feed her family."

Joe was too young to work in the fields. One of his chores was to bring a basket of food to the workers at lunchtime. One day as he trudged out to the fields, he lifted the lid and looked into the basket. On top was a chicken leg that his mother had baked the night before. Joe couldn't resist. He downed the drumstick and other food besides. When the workers took the basket from Joe, they noticed that it was lighter than usual. It didn't take them long to figure out what had happened. Joe got a serious spanking that night.

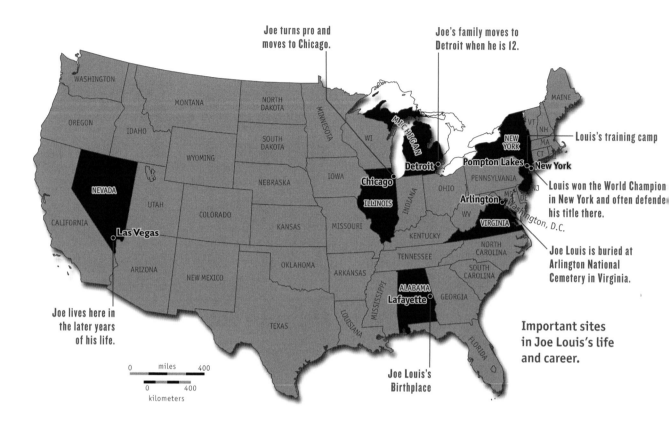

Joe turns pro and moves to Chicago.

Joe's family moves to Detroit when he is 12.

Louis's training camp

Louis won the World Champion in New York and often defended his title there.

Joe Louis is buried at Arlington National Cemetery in Virginia.

Joe lives here in the later years of his life.

Important sites in Joe Louis's life and career.

Joe Louis's Birthplace

When Joe got to be seven or eight, his older sister Eulalia began taking him to the Mt. Sinai Baptist Church, which also served as a school. Their sister Vunice, the youngest of the Barrows, went with them. Black kids from seven to seventeen attended the school—if they weren't needed for farmwork. The school had one room and two windows. There were no desks or chairs. Instead, children sat in the church pews and wrote in chalk on a blackboard. All the children brought their lunches. A big iron stove heated the room on cold days.

Joe didn't like school, mostly because he stuttered. When he spoke in class, he kept stumbling over the same sound. The other kids laughed at him. Sometimes when Eulalia took Joe to school, he refused to go in.

At about the time Joe was starting school, his mother met another sharecropper named Patrick Brooks. His wife had died, leaving him with eight children. Joe's mother and Pat Brooks eventually married. Suddenly Joe had eight stepbrothers and stepsisters. He also gained the man who became the only father he really ever had. "He was always fair and treated all those sixteen children as equally as a man could," Joe said.

When Joe's mother remarried, the fortunes of the Barrow family got better. They moved into Pat Brooks's big house. The Barrow kids could hardly believe their eyes when they saw rugs on the floors. And at a time when only a few families owned an automobile, Poppa Brooks had an early model Ford. Every Sunday, as many Brooks and Barrow kids as possible would cram themselves into the old car for a ride to church.

When Joe was about ten or eleven, he began to hear about Detroit for the first time. Two of his stepfather's older brothers had moved north and settled in Detroit. They returned to tell stories of a better life. There were jobs in Detroit for black people. Blacks were bringing home weekly paychecks from the huge Ford factory. And they didn't have to share what they earned with any landowner.

It sounded like heaven to Poppa Brooks. He decided to move north. He, Joe's mother, and his older brothers would go first. They would leave Joe's sisters and stepsisters to care for the younger children, including Joe. Once Joe's parents had gotten settled and saved enough money, they would send for the rest of the family.

Months passed. Finally, Joe's parents called upon the younger family members to join them in Detroit. The city was a place of wonder for Joe, then 12 years old. He had never seen so many people in one place. He had never seen a trolley car. Parks, libraries, movie theaters, and schoolhouses

Duffield Elementary School in Detroit was "too much for me," Joe once said. Switched to a vocational school, Joe did better.

built of brick were all new to him. He turned on his first electric light. He flushed his first toilet. The whole family got to enjoy their first radio.

Joe started going to Duffield Elementary School as a third grader. Duffield wasn't anything like the church school back in Alabama. It had hundreds of children and more classrooms than Joe could count.

Joe kept to himself. Because of his stutter, he seldom spoke in class. He spent much of his time looking out the window and wishing he were someplace else, perhaps at the movies or playing baseball, a sport he loved. He was an outstanding hitter.

His favorite activity came when school classes got together at assemblies. Because he was tall and strong for his age, his teacher asked Joe to carry the American flag. Joe's mother made sure he wore a nice starched shirt and a blue tie on those days. Carrying the flag was about the only thing about school that Joe liked.

From the beginning, Joe had trouble keeping up with other students. Before long, he found himself in classes with younger, smaller children. Even his youngest sister, Vunice, passed him.

When he was 14, one of his teachers suggested that Joe might benefit from going to a school that provided instruction in a trade. So Joe switched to Bronson Vocational School. Working with his hands, he did better. He made tables, chairs, shelves, and cabinets, all of which were put to use at home.

Meanwhile, Poppa Brooks had landed a good paying job at the Ford factory. All went well with the family for two or three years. But during the early 1930s, the nation was hit with the Great Depression. Businesses closed. Banks failed. People across the nation stopped buying automobiles. Ford and other carmakers laid off workers by the hundreds. Poppa Brooks and Joe's older brothers were among those who lost their jobs.

To help his family, Joe got a job making deliveries for a local ice company. There were no refrigerators in those days. People depended upon a sturdy wooden cabinet called an icebox to keep food from spoiling. The icebox had to be fed an almost daily supply of ice. An iceman delivered it. Joe was an iceman. He hauled big blocks of ice, some weighing as much as 50 or 60 pounds, up apartment stairs to waiting families.

While working, Joe continued to go to Bronson. There he made a new friend in Thurston McKinney, a popular student and a boxer. One day Thurston invited Joe to go to the gym. Joe had never been to a public gym before. He marveled at the sight of the boxing ring, the mats, and the punching bags of different sizes. On another visit, McKinney loaned Joe some trunks and a pair of sneakers, and Joe started punching a bag.

Before long, Joe was spending all of his spare time at the gym. Friends he made there gave Joe tips on some of boxing's basic moves. They showed him how to throw jabs—quick, straight blows—with his left hand. They showed him how to deliver a cross—a powerpacked, right-hand punch that travels rod-straight to its target. He learned how to dodge and block opponents' punches.

His mother and three of his four sisters pose with the 21-year-old Louis on a visit to his training camp in June 1935.

Background: downtown Detroit, Michigan, circa 1937.

Louis (second from right) poses with other young boxers, all members of Chicago's Golden Gloves team in 1934.

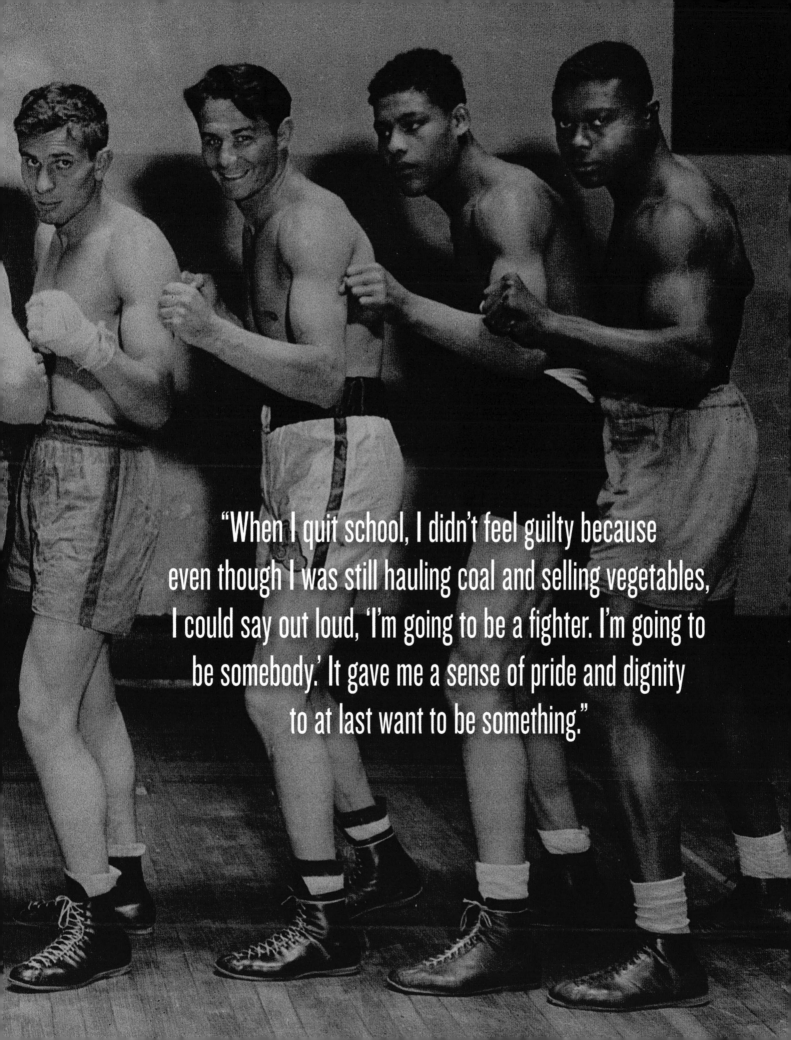

"When I quit school, I didn't feel guilty because even though I was still hauling coal and selling vegetables, I could say out loud, 'I'm going to be a fighter. I'm going to be somebody.' It gave me a sense of pride and dignity to at last want to be something."

As he improved, Joe realized that boxing made him feel good about himself. It didn't matter that he was taller than most kids his age. In the gym, there were boxers bigger than he was, and no one laughed at them. It didn't matter that he stuttered and didn't talk much. In the gym, Joe could let his fists do his talking.

Joe began spending more and more time at the gym. When he wasn't at school or working, he was skipping rope, punching bags, or boxing with light blows, called sparring.

At 17, Joe dropped out of school to devote even more time to boxing. Thurston was seldom far from his side. He explained to Joe that once he began taking part in actual bouts, he would be an amateur. As such, he would not be permitted to accept prize money. But he would receive traveling expenses and certificates that could be traded for merchandise. These were worth as much as $25 and could be exchanged for food. Joe knew his family would love getting the certificates.

Joe continued to improve and his confidence kept building. One day he told his trainers at the gym that he felt that he was ready for his first amateur fight. The gym owner arranged a bout for Joe with Johnny Miler. Later in 1932, Miler was to become a member of the U.S. Olympic boxing team. He was tough and ring wise.

The Golden Gloves trophy that Louis won.

Some of Joe's gym friends thought that Miler was clearly the better fighter. They felt that Joe needed more experience. And they were right. The match was supposed to last three rounds. It was over in two. In those two rounds, Miler knocked Joe down seven times.

The beating was not only physically painful for Joe; it hurt his pride. He felt embarrassed. He stayed away from the gym for two months, and then managed to get a job at the Ford plant. There Joe earned $25 a week for pushing truck bodies onto the assembly line.

Since Poppa Brooks had no job, the money was important to the family. But Joe hated the work. After two months, he quit to go back to the gym.

Joe trained harder than ever. In his second amateur bout, he scored a first round knockout. He then went on to win his next 13 bouts. At 19, Joe was becoming a young star.

One day Joe was asked to fill out an entry form for an upcoming fight. He wrote his name slowly and in big letters, using up an entire line with "Joe Louis." There was no room for "Barrow."

"That's OK," said the fight promoter. "Don't worry about the 'Barrow.'" He snatched the form away from Joe.

That night he fought as Joe Louis for the first time. He liked the name. One of his sisters embroidered "Joe Louis" on the back of his favorite jacket. Joe wore the jacket everywhere. It was as Joe Louis that he entered the Golden Gloves, a series of amateur boxing tournaments. Soon everyone knew him as Joe Louis.

Joe began traveling. He went to Chicago, Boston, Toronto, Canada, and other cities to face local boxers. "These were really tough guys," Joe recalled. But Joe was able to win more bouts than he lost.

Being away from the family felt strange to Joe, but he liked it. The other boxers and trainers became his friends. It was like a new family for him.

One day, a friend brought a tall, heavyset, stylishly dressed, light-skinned black man to the gym to meet Joe. His name was John Roxborough. His gentlemanly ways impressed Joe. Roxborough told Joe that he liked the way he fought. He said he might be interested in becoming Joe's manager.

Knockout
a punch that renders an opponent unconscious or unable to rise before being counted out

★ ★ ★

Promoter
a person who arranges boxing matches and provides expense money for amateurs and prize money for professionals

John Roxborough was a hero in Detroit's black community. His brother was a lawyer and state senator; his nephew, a diplomat. Roxborough was active in civic organizations and black charities. He was known to have helped a dozen or so young black men and women make their way through the University of Michigan.

Roxborough had a real estate company and an insurance business. But most of his income came from running his own numbers operation. Popular in big-city neighborhoods, the numbers game was an illegal lottery in which small bets— some no bigger than a penny or a nickel—were made on a three-digit number that appeared in local newspapers each day. A winning ten-cent bet could be worth several hundred dollars. The numbers business had made Roxborough a wealthy man. It had also gained him the social standing of a doctor or lawyer.

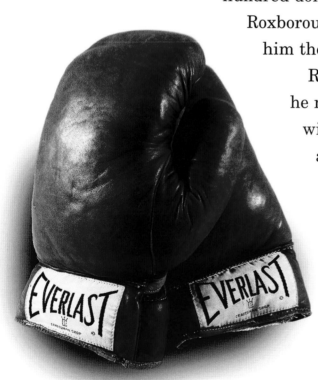

A pair of Louis's boxing gloves from the early 1940s

Roxborough told Joe that as a black fighter he needed a black manager. Black fighters with white managers were often taken advantage of, Roxborough said. They were matched against white fighters who were much better and more experienced than they were. Blacks got used up before they got a chance to achieve anything.

Joe agreed to take on Roxborough as his manager. That meant Roxborough would pay Joe's expenses and provide him with spending money. Joe agreed to split whatever prize money he earned with Roxborough on a 50-50 basis.

Once he teamed with Roxborough,

Louis (center), at his Pompton Lakes training camp, poses with the men steering his career: (left to right); Julian Black, assistant manager; Jack Blackburn, Louis's trainer; Louis; John Roxborough, manager; and Russell Cowan, who tutored Louis in grade school subjects.

Joe's life quickly changed. The two went to a local sporting goods store, and Roxborough told the owner to give Joe whatever he wanted. Joe was delighted to pick out brand new shoes, trunks, and professional boxing gloves. Roxborough also provided Joe with five dollars every Saturday as pocket money.

Early in 1934, Joe won the Detroit amateur heavyweight title. Roxborough spoke to him afterward. "I think you're ready," he said. "Time to turn professional." Then Roxborough explained that he wanted Joe to move to Chicago and continue his career there under the watchful eye of Julian Black, who would become Joe's manager in partnership with Roxborough. Joe liked the idea of becoming a professional. It meant that instead of bringing home trophies and merchandise certificates, Joe would

Lightweight
a professional boxer
weighing up to
135 pounds

★ ★ ★

Rubdown
rubbing and patting
the body to increase
circulation and
to relieve tension

be earning prize money. But he felt uneasy about moving to Chicago. It would be hard to leave his family and friends.

A few days later, Joe and Roxborough spoke again, and Joe agreed to the plan—with one condition. "OK, I'm ready," he told Roxborough, "but you'll have to tell Momma." Roxborough visited Joe's home and sat down with his mother. He promised her that her son would live well and lead a good life in Chicago. His mother agreed to let him go. "I would have gone anyway," Joe said, "but now I could go with an easy conscience."

When Joe's train from Detroit arrived in Chicago, Julian Black was waiting for him. Stocky, with slicked-down hair and a gruff manner, Black took Joe to the apartment house where he would be living. It was the first time in his life that Joe had a room of his own.

Later, Black took Joe to Trafton's Gym. There he sought out Jack, who was to be Joe's trainer. At first glance, Joe didn't know what to make of Jack Blackburn. He was tall and wiry, with a shaved head and a long scar running down one side of his face. He gave Joe the creeps. Blackburn had a background to match his hard appearance. Earlier, as a top-ranked lightweight boxer, Blackburn had had more than 100 bouts, and he had won most of them. He also had been in and out of prison several times. Back in Detroit, Joe was able to kid and clown around with his friends as he trained. But one look at Blackburn, and Joe knew that pro boxing was going to be serious business.

Blackburn set up a strict schedule for Joe to follow. Each morning before sunrise Joe was to run six miles in a nearby park. Then it was back to his apartment for breakfast.

After breakfast, Joe had a nap. He spent most of the rest of the day in the gym. In their training sessions, Blackburn wouldn't allow Joe to enter the ring. Instead, he made Joe throw punches at the heavy bag while he watched.

Blackburn could see at once that Joe was off balance when he delivered a punch. He made Joe plant his feet firmly to get more muscle into his punches.

One day in the gym while Blackburn was giving Joe a rubdown, he spoke to him in serious tones and explained that, as a black, Joe's chances for real success in boxing were limited. "The white man ain't too keen on it," he said. "You have to really be something to get anywhere. If you really ain't gonna be another Jack Johnson, you got some hope."

Joe knew all about Jack Johnson. Smart and fearless, Johnson had been the world's first black heavyweight champion. He held the title from 1908 to 1915. During those years he was the most famous black man in America.

But people didn't think of Johnson merely in terms of his boxing skill. He was more notable for the way he lived his life. Johnson resisted the harsh system of racial segregation. He simply refused to live as a second-class citizen. Johnson owned a Chicago nightclub, had his own jazz band, and drove a dazzling yellow sports car. In the ring, he would often taunt opponents and gloat over his victories. Worst of all—at least to white

Jack Johnson, the first African American to win the world's heavyweight championship

Background: A poster for a heavyweight championship fight between Johnson and James J. Jeffries, held in Reno, Nevada, on July 4, 1910

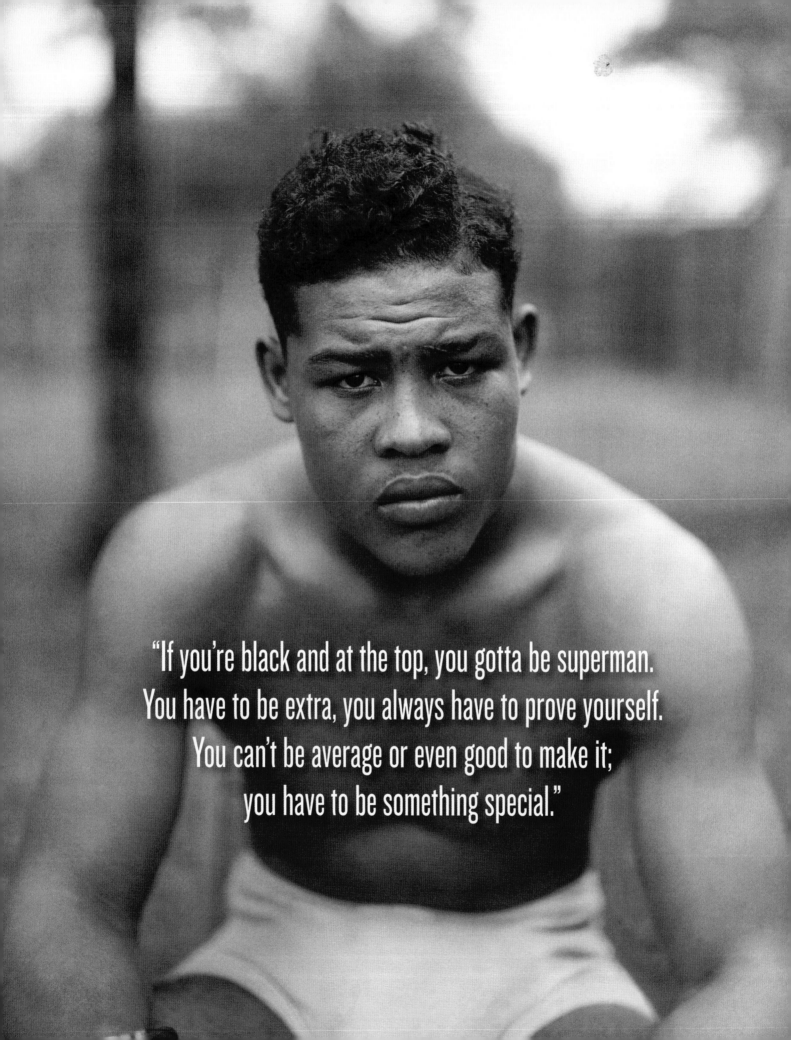

"If you're black and at the top, you gotta be superman. You have to be extra, you always have to prove yourself. You can't be average or even good to make it; you have to be something special."

Americans—he openly dated white women.

Johnson eventually lost his title to big, strong Jess Willard in a fight held in Havana, Cuba. Incredibly, the bout went 26 rounds. (Boxing rules now limit fights to 15 rounds.) Willard was white. The men who controlled boxing had no intention of letting the heavyweight title fall into the hands of another black boxer, especially one who spoke his mind and refused to be treated as an inferior. Again and again, Louis was told. "Don't be another Jack Johnson."

Roxborough had advice for Joe, too. "To be a champion, you've got to be a gentleman first," he told Joe. "We never, never say anything bad about an opponent. Before a fight, you say how great you think he is; after a fight, you say how great you thought he was."

"And for God's sake," Roxborough added, "after you beat a white opponent, don't smile."

Joe heeded the advice. In the years that followed, Joe would often be described as the "deadpan" champion. That meant that he usually wore a serious, even solemn expression. Even after a victory, there would seldom be any sign of joy.

By now Roxborough and his team realized that Joe was a rare specimen. He had every punch—a powerful jab, an uppercut, and a left hook. His right cross, delivered over his opponent's lead, was also deadly. And with his great hand speed, Louis was able to put together his punches in lethal combinations. The team felt certain that he could become the world's heavyweight champion — as long as he followed the rules they had laid down.

> **Uppercut**
> an upward punch delivered from about waist level
>
> ★ ★ ★
>
> **Hook**
> a short punch delivered with a circular motion
>
> ★ ★ ★
>
> **Combination**
> a series of rapidly delivered punches

In mid-August 1936, shortly before defeating Jack Sharkey, Louis has a cold stare for the camera.

Joe's first fight as a professional was set for July 4, 1934. Jack Kracken, a leading Chicago heavyweight, was his opponent. In the days before the bout, Blackburn kept telling Joe that he would be at a disadvantage because he was a black fighter going up against a white fighter. In a close fight, both he and Joe knew that the white judges would be inclined to cast their votes for the white boxer. Joe must go for a knockout.

In the dressing room before the fight, Joe was nervous. And when he entered the ring and looked over at his opponent, he got even more jittery. Kracken had black hair and wore white trunks. He looked older than Joe. He seemed confident. Joe did have a weight advantage, however. Kracken tipped the scales at 175. Joe weighed 181.

The bell rang. Joe moved briskly to the center of the ring and began pounding away at Kracken's ribs. He forgot about being nervous. When Kracken dropped his guard to protect his body, Joe belted him with a left to the chin. Kracken went down and did not get up until the count of nine. On their next exchange, Joe knocked Kracken out of the ring. The fight had not lasted two minutes.

Afterward, Joe got his first check as a professional boxer—$59. To Joe, that was good money for two minutes work. Roxborough refused to take his share and told Joe to keep the whole amount. Joe sent most of the money home to his mother but kept some to celebrate with. That meant going bowling and gobbling down junk food with Freddie Guinyard, an old pal from Detroit.

Joe went on to win his first four pro fights, three of them by knockouts. As he kept winning, his popularity built. People began to stop in at the gym and watch him train. Once, during a sparring session, Joe happened to catch a glimpse of a pretty, well-dressed young woman among the spectators. "Classy looking" is the way Joe described her. The woman was Marva Trotter, Joe found out.

In December 1934, Joe knocked out Lee Ramage, a fine Los Angeles heavyweight, in the third round of a bout held at the Chicago Stadium. The win gave him 12 victories for the year. Ten of the fights were decided by knockouts.

After the Ramage fight, Joe decided to throw a party. He asked Blackburn to invite the girl who had visited the gym. Marva arrived at the party with her sister Gladys. At 18, Marva was a couple of years younger than Joe. They talked for a long time that evening. Marva was interested in the world of fashion. She wanted to become a designer. Joe liked Marva. He had never met any woman quite like her. As for Marva, she had deeper feelings. "It was love at first sight," she later admitted. Within a year, the two would be married.

Louis with the former Marva Trotter, his bride of a few hours, shortly after his fight against Max Baer at Yankee Stadium in New York in September 1935.

By now, Louis was the sensation of the boxing world. And, as he was beginning to realize, he was also becoming an idol in the black community. On the streets of Chicago, in the city's stores, restaurants, and barbershops, black men would clap him on the back and seek to shake his hand. Women wanted to kiss him. And people would shout such things as, "You're our savior, Joe!" or "Show them whites!"

Newspaper reporters who covered his bouts coined nicknames for him. Some of the names were foolish. Others, in referring to his skin color, were offensive. Louis was called the Dark Destroyer, the Alabama Assassin, and the Coffee Colored Kayo King. One nickname stuck—the Brown Bomber.

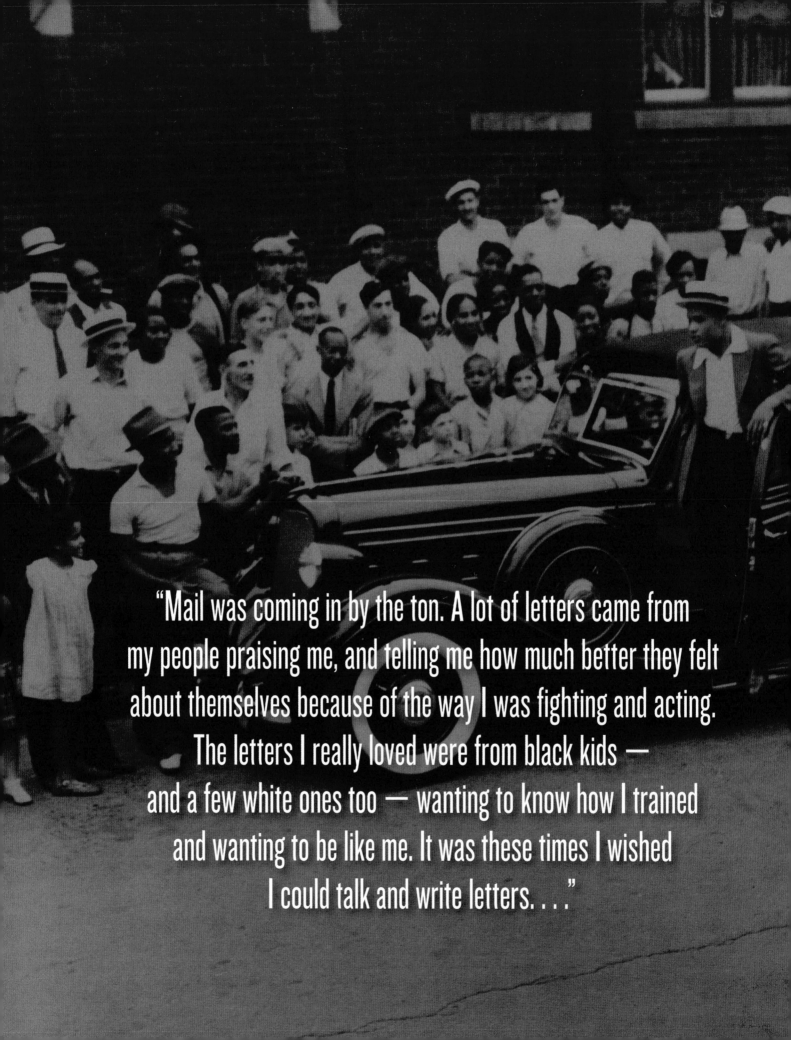

"Mail was coming in by the ton. A lot of letters came from my people praising me, and telling me how much better they felt about themselves because of the way I was fighting and acting. The letters I really loved were from black kids — and a few white ones too — wanting to know how I trained and wanting to be like me. It was these times I wished I could talk and write letters. . . ."

A crowd welcomes Louis on a return visit to the Black Bottom section of Detroit, where the Louis family lived during Joe's boyhood.

After Louis had won six more fights, Roxborough and Black felt he was ready for the big money matches in New York City. They got Joe to sign a contract with the shrewd and tough-minded Mike Jacobs, a promoter who was taking control of boxing in New York. Under the terms of the contract, Jacobs would arrange Louis's future fights. Roxborough would continue to manage Louis, but with Jacobs as his partner.

Jacobs told Louis and his trainers that getting Joe a championship bout was going to be a tough job. He said that there was an unwritten agreement among boxing promoters that there would never be another black heavyweight champion. Already, promoters were scurrying about trying to find a pale-skinned fighter who could defeat Louis and put an end to his championship dreams. They were looking for what was called a "white hope." The managers of white boxers who had little or no chance of defeating Louis were careful to avoid him. HEAVYWEIGHTS DUCKING LOUIS, declared a headline in a New York City newspaper.

Some newspapers of the time clearly reflected a racist attitude. One described Louis as "Mike Jacobs's pet pickaninny" (pickaninny was an offensive word for a black child).

Other newspapers belittled Louis by printing his speech in a dialect of the rural poor and uneducated. For example, a Chicago newspaper offered a cartoon depicting a classroom scene. Louis is one of the students. "Joseph," says the teacher, "Make me up a sentence with the word 'defeat' in it."

"Sho!" Louis replies. "I pops 'em on the chin and dey drags 'em out by de feet."

Mike Jacobs paid no attention to how the newspapers treated Louis. He realized that Joe, with his quiet and dignified manner, was becoming popular among whites as well as blacks. Jacobs wasted no time in arranging for Louis to fight Primo Carnera, an Italian fighter who had held the heavyweight championship in 1933 and 1934. With this bout,

30

Huge crowds visited Louis's training camps to watch his workouts. Here he skips rope not long before his bruising win over England's Tommy Farr.

Louis would be taking an important step in opening the door to the participation of blacks in other American sports.

The day before he left for New York and the Carnera fight, Louis turned 21. One of his sisters gave him a razor for his birthday. Louis liked the gift, although he had not yet started to shave.

From the moment Joe's train from Chicago pulled into New York, he was treated as a celebrity. The porters at the station stopped handling baggage. They swarmed into the car where Louis sat, picked him up, and carried him off the train. Afterward, a press conference at Mike Jacobs's office was jammed with reporters. Flashbulbs popped. Newsreel cameras hummed. The police had to be called to clear away the enormous crowd that gathered in the street outside.

To escape the uproar, Roxborough set up a training camp for Louis in Pompton Lakes, New Jersey, a 45-minute drive from Manhattan. Hundreds of people still showed up each day to watch Louis work out.

The ring announcer lifts Louis's hand in recognition of his victory over former heavyweight champion Primo Carnera in New York in June 1935.

On the night of the fight, more than 60,000 fans crowded into Yankee Stadium. Several special trains brought throngs of Joe's black supporters from Chicago, Detroit, Pittsburgh, Cleveland, and other cities. Joe would later call this the best night he experienced in his years of fighting.

Much of Carnera's success in the ring was due to his size. He was huge— six feet seven, 260 pounds. But Blackburn knew how to equalize the matchup. He told Louis to work on Carnera's belly. When Primo's hands came down, Joe was to switch to Carnera's head.

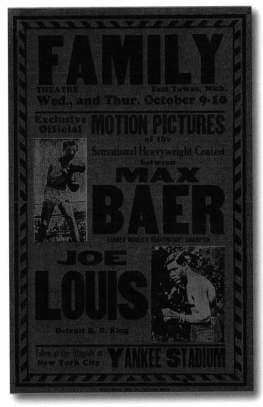

This poster promotes a newsreel showing of Louis's fight against Max Baer in September 1935.

It took a few rounds for Louis to get used to his towering opponent. Then he began to pound the big man's body and head. In the sixth round, Louis put the bloodied Carnera down three times. When the referee saw that the battered Carnera could no longer defend himself, he stopped the fight.

Afterward, a few newspapers that covered the fight continued to show their racial bias by making Louis sound simple and poorly educated. According to the *Washington Post*, when he was asked how he managed to overpower Carnera, Louis replied, "I jes' kept on hittin' him till he quit."

Following his victory, Louis was given time to visit Marva Trotter in Chicago and his family in Detroit. A few weeks later, he returned to New York for his next big fight. This time he was matched against hard-punching Max Baer. Like Carnera, Baer had once held the heavyweight title.

A few days before the bout with Max Baer, Marva, her sister, and her brother arrived in New York. Joe and Marva planned on getting married in a few weeks. But Joe decided he didn't want to wait.

"I've always considered the Baer fight my greatest. I've never had better hand speed; I felt so good I knew I could have fought for two or three days straight."

Louis's left jab finds its target in his bout with Max Baer in September 1935.

Through most of his adult life, Louis was an avid golfer. He especially liked to play in the rain.

He wanted to get married right away. The wedding was hurriedly planned for the same day as the Baer fight. There was no time for flowers, music, or a wedding cake. Early in the evening, Marva's brother, a minister from Iowa, performed the ceremony at an apartment in Harlem. After Joe kissed the bride, he was whisked from the apartment and into a waiting limousine. Police squad cars, their sirens blaring, sped the bridegroom across the Harlem River to Yankee Stadium. When Louis climbed through the ropes, more than 85,000 fans stood and cheered and applauded. Joe hardly noticed. He was peeking at Marva in her ringside seat.

The fight didn't last long. Louis nailed Baer with a solid right uppercut in the first round. He had Baer bleeding in round two. In the third, Louis sent Baer to the canvas twice. In the fourth, he finished matters with a left hook and a right to the head. After the fight, Louis celebrated with Marva, her family, his managers and trainers, and a few friends. He was a happy man that night. He had a wife whom he was crazy about. He had fame. He had more money than he ever dreamed of having. Black Americans were inspired by Louis. He held the promise of better times.

More and more, Jacobs and Roxborough talked about getting Louis a chance to fight for the heavyweight title, then held by James J. Braddock. But standing between Louis and the title was a 32-year-old German fighter named Max Schmeling. After winning several German titles, he had come to New York to continue his career. He captured the heavyweight championship in 1930 and then lost it two years later. Now he wanted it back. He saw Louis as a stepping-stone to a title fight against Braddock. Mike Jacobs arranged for Louis to take on Schmeling in the spring of 1936.

Schmeling had seen the Louis-Baer fight and had noticed something. After Louis jabbed with his left, he dropped his left hand low. That created a big opening for a right hand. And Schmeling had a good right. "I guarantee you," Schmeling said, "if Louis makes the same mistakes with me that he did with Baer, I shall knock him out!"

Louis laughed when he read what Schmeling had said. He had no fear of the German boxer. After all, he had fought 27 times as a professional. No one had beaten him. He had not the slightest doubt he would win.

But, as one reporter noted, Louis seemed "too sure of himself for his own good." He did not appear in top form. In practice sessions in the ring, he looked lifeless. His punches lacked power. His timing was off.

To some, it seemed almost as if Louis had lost interest in boxing. Joe did, in fact, have another great love—golf. Time after time, he would cut short a workout and slip off to the golf course.

Blackburn was upset. He told Louis he was making a big mistake. The muscles he used to swing a golf club were different from those used to punch someone. Louis ignored Blackburn. He felt certain he would win, golf or no golf.

In Yankee Stadium on the night of the fight, Blackburn was worried. Just before the bell rang for the first round, he warned Joe of Schmeling's dangerous right hand. "For God's sake," he said, "keep your left arm high."

Joe jabbed away at Schmeling as the bout got underway, hitting him easily. He got more confident. The second round brought more of the same.

Movie theater newsreels featured round-by-round coverage of Schmeling's upset win over Joe Louis in June 1936.

But midway through the round, Joe dropped his left hand to throw a hook. Schmeling saw the opening. He clubbed Joe with a right hand that landed on his chin. The punch staggered Louis. Everything got blurry. He barely managed to stay on his feet until the bell sounded, ending the round.

In the fourth round, Joe repeated the mistake. Schmeling was ready. He jolted Louis with a right hand to the jaw. Joe went down. It was the first time he had ever been knocked off his feet as a professional. He thought his jaw was broken.

The fight continued for several more rounds. But Joe fought in a fog. His punches had no power. Schmeling kept shooting hard right hands to Joe's head and body. He knocked him out in the 12th round. Joe had to be carried to the dressing room.

In the days that followed, Joe's wounds healed. But the damage to his pride was long lasting. In the few years that he had been boxing, Joe had become an important figure in the black community as a symbol of racial progress. Joe realized that in losing he had let not only himself down.

When Louis was knocked out by Max Schmeling in June 1936, he felt he had let not only himself down, but all African Americans as well.

He had failed to live up to the expectations of what he called "a whole race of people." He felt ashamed.

While Joe was healing in mind and body, Jacobs and Roxborough were busy. Both were eager to get Louis back into the ring. They arranged for him to fight Jack Sharkey, another former heavyweight champion.

At training camp, Blackburn did everything he could to make certain Joe would be ready for Sharkey. He would not let Joe out of his sight. He barred the public from attending training sessions. Only the press was allowed to watch. Reporters saw the "old" Louis. He worked hard. Golf? Forget about it.

The fight was staged at Yankee Stadium on an August night in 1936. Blackburn told Joe that Sharkey would try to use the same tactics that had worked for Schmeling—and he did. Sharkey threw one right hand after another. Joe blocked most of them. In the second round, Joe

Exhibition
a boxing bout staged for
the public with the fighters
not trying their hardest
to win and usually with
no recognition of a winner

answered one of Sharkey's rights with a right hand of his own, and Sharkey went down. He knocked Sharkey out with another right hand in the third round.

"Joe's mad at Schmeling," Blackburn told the press after the fight, "but Sharkey paid for it."

So did a string of other fighters. After Joe's victory over Sharkey, Roxborough and Jacobs booked Joe for a series of 10 fights, four of which were exhibitions. He won all ten, nine by knockouts.

Joe still wanted to fight Max Schmeling. But when Mike Jacobs offered the German $300,000 to fight Louis, Schmeling turned down the offer. What Schmeling was hoping for was a chance to fight Braddock for the heavyweight championship. At the same time, Mike was also trying to lure Braddock into the ring as an opponent for Louis.

Jacobs's efforts paid off. The 32-year-old Braddock agreed to defend his title against Louis, who had just turned 23. Louis was the youngest man to challenge for the championship in boxing history. June 22, 1937, was set as the date for the fight. Comiskey Park in Chicago, a baseball stadium, was to be the site.

Until he won the heavyweight title in 1935, Braddock had never been looked upon as anything more than an average fighter. He had lost more bouts than he had won. But he was tough and experienced.

At the opening bell, Braddock took charge. He nailed Louis with a hard right hand that floored him. But Joe bounced right back up. Before the round ended, he had Braddock's left eye bleeding.

For the rest of the bout, Louis was in command. Braddock grew weary. His legs wobbled. Blackburn, however, warned Joe to be cautious.

The fight ended in the eighth round. Louis delivered a right hook to Braddock's jaw. The champion landed on his face and did not move as the referee counted him out.

"The one-time cotton picker was now the Heavyweight Champion of the entire world."

In their match for the heavyweight title, Louis knocked out Braddock in the eighth round with an explosive right hook. Here referee Tommy Thomas directs Louis to a neutral corner of the ring as Braddock lifts his head from the canvas.

Background: Huge headlines in the *Detroit Times*, an African-American newspaper, hail Louis's victory over Braddock.

Following his victory over Louis in June 1936, Max Schmeling and his wife, Anny Ondra, were greeted by German chancellor Adolph Hitler.

"A new world's champion!" radio reporter Clem McCarthy cried into his microphone. "Joe Louis is the new world's champion!"

Black America celebrated that night. In Chicago, bonfires lit the streets as a huge throng paraded. In Detroit, a large crowd had gathered outside the home of Louis's mother. They listened to the radio account of the fight over a loudspeaker. When Braddock went down, they filled the night sky with their cheers. In New York, a multitude of Joe's Harlem fans marched down Seventh Avenue chanting, "We want Schmeling!"

Louis wanted Schmeling, too, and in the worst way. His loss to the German boxer in 1936 was the only blot on his record.

Schmeling was just as eager for the rematch. It was the only chance he had to win back the championship.

Once the contracts were signed, the Louis-Schmeling fight took shape as one of the most notable sports events of the 20th century. It was not merely a boxing match, two fighters squaring off for an important title. In the spring of 1938, as the date of the bout drew near, Europe was in turmoil. World War II was on the horizon. Adolph Hitler and his Nazi Party had taken control in Germany. With his powerful army and air force, Hitler was eager for conquest. Within a year, he would order the invasion of Poland. His armies would occupy most of Europe before the decade ended.

Hitler and the Nazis believed that their "Aryan" race was superior to all others. Their racist policy would bring death to 11 million people, including 6 million Jews. That slaughter is now known as the Holocaust.

After Schmeling had defeated Louis two years before, he had become a favorite of Hitler's and a symbol of Nazi Germany. Hitler congratulated Schmeling for his "splendid victory" and sent a huge bouquet of flowers to the boxer's wife.

Just as Schmeling stood for Germany, Louis came to represent America and anti-Nazi feeling in the United States. His role was made clear when he was invited to the White House to meet President Franklin D. Roosevelt. Roosevelt felt Joe's upper arm and said, "Joe, we're depending on those muscles for America."

"Let me tell you, that was a thrill," Joe said afterward. "Now, even more, I knew I had to get Schmeling good . . . the whole damn country was depending on me."

Louis also had personal reasons for wanting to subdue Schmeling. He recalled that in their first fight he had been the victim of a late hit. Schmeling had sent a hard right cross crashing into Joe's jaw just as the bell had ended the fifth round or a split second after it had sounded. Joe had been dazed by the illegal punch. The memory of it made Joe vengeful. In addition, Blackburn kept telling Joe that Hitler and the Nazis looked upon blacks as inferior to whites. "I don't like Schmeling because his people don't like my people," Joe said.

In the weeks before the fight, Blackburn created a new strategy for Louis. He wanted Joe to start fast, to come out of his corner swinging.

In their second bout, a globally important event, Louis wasted no time avenging himself for his earlier defeat at the hands of Max Schmeling.

Background: Although the U.S. was suffering the effects of the Great Depression, people spent nearly a million dollars buying tickets for the Louis-Schmeling rematch. That had rarely happened before in the history of boxing.

He didn't intend to give Schmeling the time to plant his feet and start throwing punches. He wanted Joe on top of his rival from the opening bell.

The radio broadcast of Louis's bout with Schmeling reached thousands of his fans in New York's Harlem.

When the day of the fight arrived, Joe felt completely confident. A friend asked him, "How do you feel, Joe?"

"I'm scared," he said.

"Scared?"

Joe grinned. "Yeah," he said, "I'm scared I might kill Schmeling tonight."

People swarmed into New York by car, train, and plane. A special boat ferried fans from Boston. Hotels and guesthouses were filled to overflowing. In Harlem's Hotel Theresa, beds were put in the lobby to handle the crush of guests.

At Yankee Stadium on the night of the fight, Louis was the first to enter the ring. Blackburn was at his side, encouraging him to keep moving, keep dancing. Joe said he was "rarin' to go." The fans applauded as Schmeling, surrounded by police, walked down the aisle and climbed into the ring. He stood quietly, his hands at his sides, and stared at Louis.

All across the country people tuned in on their radios. With more than 60 million Americans listening, it would be one of the biggest radio audiences in history.

"They're ready with the bell just about to ring," the radio audience heard the gruff-voiced Clem McCarthy say. When it rang, the huge crowed roared and people leaned forward in their seats. Schmeling, grinning slightly, walked out of his corner. Louis, who usually started slowly, rushed toward Schmeling and stung him with a quick left jab. Louis followed with two more jabs, then a left to the body. Schmeling backed into the ropes while trying to defend himself. Louis pounded him with rights and lefts to the head and body. "Move, Max, move!" someone shouted from Schmeling's corner.

The two men clinched. When they came out of it, Louis caught Schmeling with two more lefts and a right to the head. After another barrage of punches, Schmeling lurched back. He was hurt. Then Louis threw a long right hand that landed on Schmeling's side. The German shrieked in pain.

Louis followed with several punches to the face. Schmeling grabbed the ropes. The referee waved Joe away from his helpless opponent and started counting. But Schmeling staggered forward at the count of two. Joe caught him with a left hook and a right cross. Schmeling fell to his knees. The crowd was on its feet and screaming.

Schmeling got up. He went down again and got up again. Louis moved in. McCarthy described what happened next: "A right to the body! A left to the jaw! And Schmeling is down!"

On his hands and knees, Schmeling tried to stand up. The referee counted to five, but no further. Seeing that Schmeling was whipped and unable to defend himself, he stopped the fight. "The fight is over . . . " said Clem McCarthy. "Max Schmeling is beaten in one round!"

In black homes and neighborhoods, Louis's stunning victory set off celebrations that lasted for hours. Author Richard Wright described the scene in New York's Harlem, where people took over the streets: "They shouted, sang, laughed, yelled, blew paper horns, clasped hands, and formed weaving snake-lines, whistled, sounded sirens, and honked auto horns."

In Detroit, thousands marched and chanted, "Joe knocked out Hitler cold!" In Philadelphia, police tried to keep the crowd orderly but gave up. They folded their arms and watched. "Boy, am I glad Joe Louis doesn't fight every night in the week," said a Newark, New Jersey, policeman in the midst of the partying.

African-American newspaper reporters spoke of the fight's social impact. Frank Marshall Davis of the *American Negro Press* called it a victory for the nation's 14 million black Americans. The *Philadelphia Independent* said that Louis, in defeating Schmeling, had created more goodwill for American blacks than anything since the Civil War.

Joe was now at the very peak of his career. "I had the championship and I had beaten the man who had humiliated me," he said. "America was proud of me, my people were proud of me. . . ."

In the years following his victory over Schmeling, Joe's managers kept him busy. Almost every heavyweight who wanted a chance to take the title away from Louis was given that chance. None succeeded.

In 1941, Louis fought seven times. Most fights he won easily. One exception was a bout with Billy Conn. Louis was the winner, but it was no cinch. Younger than Louis, fast, with lightning punches, Conn outboxed Louis for 12 rounds. But in the 13th round, Conn got careless and left an opening.

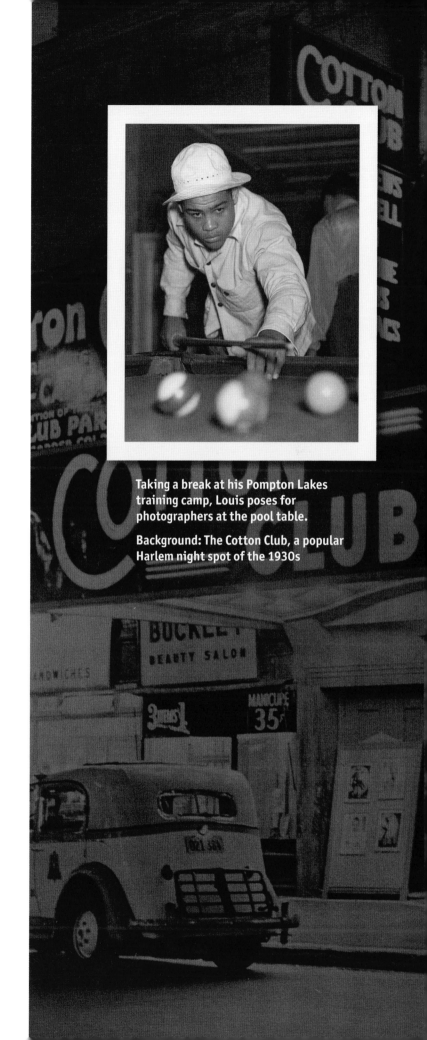

Taking a break at his Pompton Lakes training camp, Louis poses for photographers at the pool table.

Background: The Cotton Club, a popular Harlem night spot of the 1930s

Surrounded by a cluster of New York police officers and surging admirers, Louis makes his way to the dressing room at Yankee Stadium following his win over Max Schmeling.

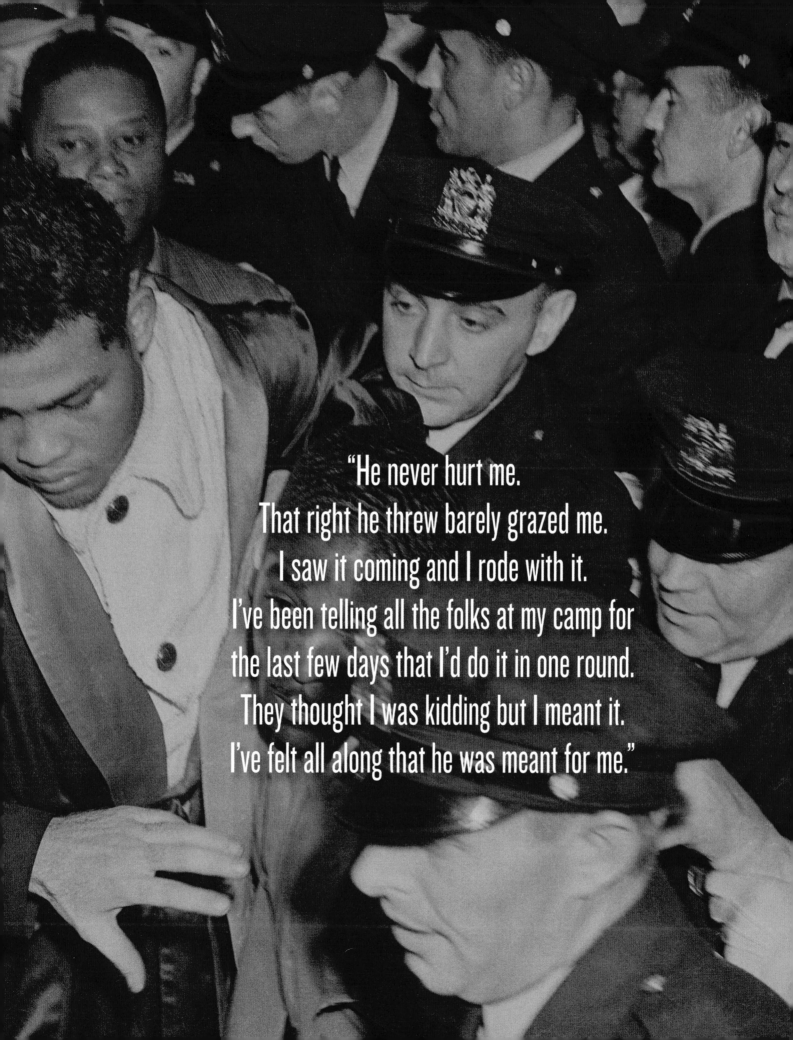

"He never hurt me.
That right he threw barely grazed me.
I saw it coming and I rode with it.
I've been telling all the folks at my camp for
the last few days that I'd do it in one round.
They thought I was kidding but I meant it.
I've felt all along that he was meant for me."

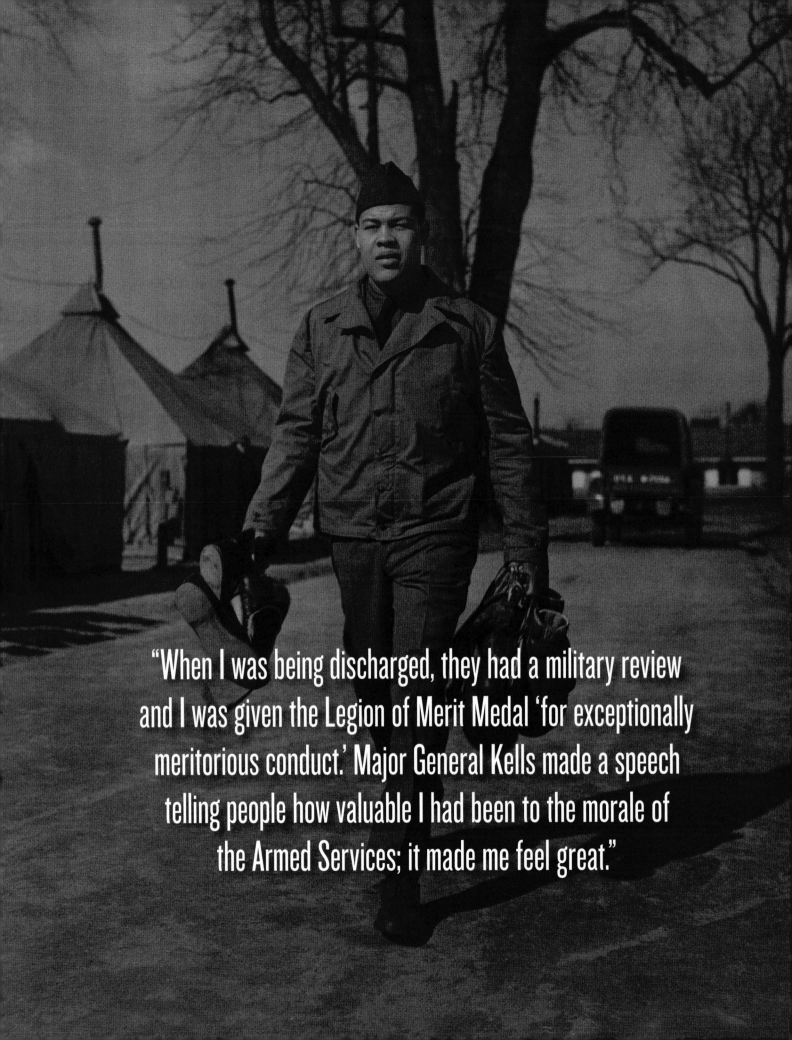

"When I was being discharged, they had a military review and I was given the Legion of Merit Medal 'for exceptionally meritorious conduct.' Major General Kells made a speech telling people how valuable I had been to the morale of the Armed Services; it made me feel great."

Louis unleashed a right hook that connected with Conn's jaw. With two seconds left in the round, Conn was counted out.

Before the year ended, Louis's life, and everyone else's, changed for all time. On December 7, 1941, Japanese planes attacked Pearl Harbor, Hawaii. The United States was plunged into World War II. Joe did what millions of his fellow citizens did — he joined the army.

The army had no intention of sending Joe to fight in Europe or the Pacific. Instead, he was used to help build soldiers' confidence and to boost their spirits. He did so by visiting countless military bases, usually taking part in boxing exhibitions.

Louis had two championship bouts during this time. Both of them were for charitable causes. In one, he donated his earnings to the Navy Relief Society. The organization aided the families of navy personnel killed during the war. The second fight was for the benefit of the Army Relief Fund. Newspapers hailed Joe for his patriotism. His generosity served to boost Joe's stature as white America's first black hero.

During World War II, the army was just as segregated as schools and restaurants in the Deep South. Black soldiers were made to serve in separate units under white officers. As an enlisted man, Joe had more than a few brushes with discrimination.

In one of Joe's army boxing exhibitions, black troops were given the worst seats, far back in the arena. Louis protested and said he wasn't going to box. "I'm not going to box," he told the commanding officer. The officer got the message. Black soldiers were moved closer to the action.

At Fort Riley, Kansas, Joe met Jackie Robinson, who was stationed there. The two became close friends. In 1947, Robinson became Major League Baseball's first African-American player.

Carrying boxing gloves and shoes, Louis heads for his training quarters at Fort Dix, New Jersey, to prepare for his bout with Abe Simon at Madison Square Garden in New York on March 27, 1942. The event was staged for the benefit of the Army Relief Fund.

Robinson told Joe that he wanted to attain a position of authority in the army; he wanted to become an officer. To do so, Robinson would have to attend the army's Officer's Candidate School. But, as Robinson explained, the army would not accept his application. Seventeen other African-American soldiers had the same problem.

Joe called an official in Washington who happened to be a good friend. He looked into the situation. As a result, Jackie Robinson and the other African-American soldiers were admitted to Officer's Candidate School. Robinson came out of the army as a lieutenant. Joe felt proud about that.

Joe, who attained the rank of technical sergeant, was given overseas duty in 1944. He put on boxing exhibitions for troops in Italy, North Africa, and England. In October 1945, a month after the war ended, Joe was discharged from the army. He was 31. Military service had taken up four years of his life.

Everything was different now. His old team was gone. Jack Blackburn, Joe's trainer, had died during the war. Joe's mother was gone, too. John Roxborough was serving a prison sentence for his involvement in illegal gambling.

In 1945, Marva had ended her marriage to Joe by divorcing him. The couple remarried a year later. They divorced a second time in 1949. This time there was no remarriage. Joe and Marva had two children. A daughter, Jacquelin, arrived in 1943. A son, Joe Jr., was born in 1947. Joe was not an ideal father. Always traveling, he seldom saw his children.

After World War II, Joe's biggest problem was lack of money. He always liked to enjoy himself. He liked flashy clothes, pretty women, and good times. He admitted that he spent whatever he earned as if it were never going to stop. He owned 25 pairs of shoes and 20 suits. He bought a home for his mother and a horse farm for himself and Marva outside of Detroit. He gave his sister Emmarell the money to open a hat shop. When his sister

Louis survived being knocked to the canvas to win a disputed decision over Jersey Joe Walcott in their championship bout at Madison Square Garden in December 1947.

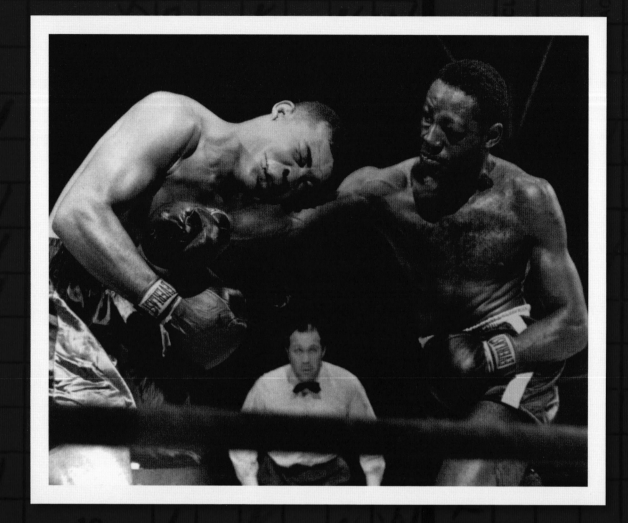

"My crazy little world was crumbling all around me now.
Nothing left for me to do, so in the middle of the summer,
I announced that I'd decided to come out of
retirement and challenge Ezzard Charles for the championship.
The reason—taxes."

Vunice wanted to go to Howard University in Washington, D.C., Joe paid all of her expenses. He sponsored the Black Bomber softball team for his buddies in Detroit. The team toured far and wide. Joe paid the bills. Countless friends and relatives asked him for money and got it. "They should have called him 'Can't-say-no Joe,'" a friend noted.

Louis has a hug for contestants at the Miss Paris beauty contest, held at the Hotel Claridge in Paris in April 1948.

To earn money, Louis defended his title several times. He beat Billy Conn in a rematch. He defeated the cagey Jersey Joe Walcott twice.

Although he was still winning, Joe knew his skills were beginning to decline. Training for bouts was not fun anymore. He began to think about quitting boxing. In March 1949, he made it official and announced his retirement as the undefeated heavyweight champion of the world.

But Joe still had a problem. In the years when he was earning big money, sometimes he had failed to pay his income taxes. To earn the hundreds of thousands of dollars that he owed, Joe felt his only choice was to come out of retirement and to fight again. At Yankee Stadium in New York on a cool and cloudy September night in 1950, Joe Louis faced Ezzard Charles, a clever boxer who was seven years younger than Louis. Charles had replaced Louis as the heavyweight champion.

Once the fight began, it was plain that this was not the Joe Louis of old. He was slow and acted weary. Ezzard Charles quickly took charge.

Ezzard Charles (right) took over as heavyweight champion after Louis retired. Louis sought to win his title back from Charles in September 1950.

Background: Judges record each boxer's points for every round of a fight.

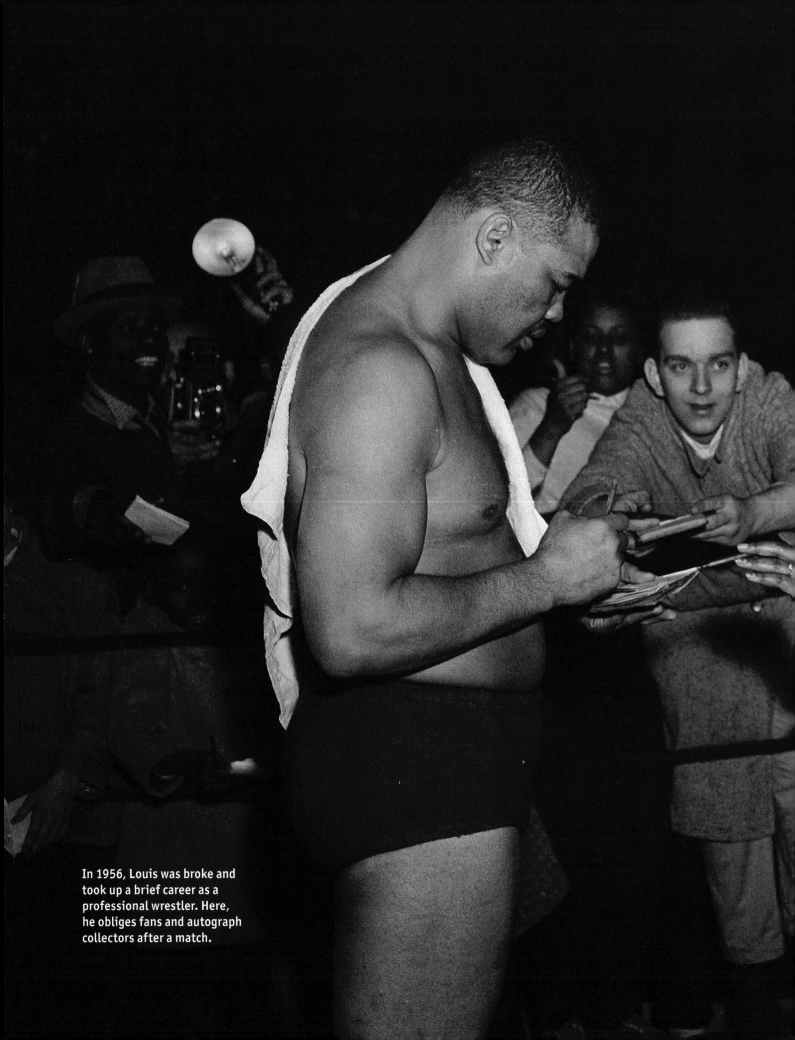

In 1956, Louis was broke and took up a brief career as a professional wrestler. Here, he obliges fans and autograph collectors after a match.

The papers and magazines had all kinds of articles about my tax problems. Fans were sending me money in the mail. Even kids were sending me dollars out of the little money they saved. One little kid even mailed me a dime."

A 20-foot-long bronze sculpture in the form of an awesome fist and forearm stands in Detroit's Hart Plaza in honor of Louis.

He jolted Louis with quick jabs and smashing right-hand punches. By the fifth round, Louis's left eye was swollen almost shut.

Between rounds, Louis sat silently on his stool, his head bowed. Sweat glistened on his brown shoulders and arms. He had once been hailed as the greatest heavyweight champion of all time. Now it was clear that his days of glory were over.

In the 14th round, Charles staggered Louis with a powerful uppercut. Joe stumbled and grabbed a rope with one hand to keep from falling. When the bell sounded for the 15th round, Louis was exhausted. Bruised and bleeding, he had to be helped to his feet. He managed to last until the round's end. The judges' decision was no surprise. It went to Charles.

What happened in the ring that night saddened millions. And poor Charles; instead of being hailed in victory, fans showed him disrespect. When he returned to his home in Cincinnati, black youngsters jeered him. "It didn't matter that Charles was black," said sportswriter Jimmie Cannon. "He had beaten Louis and they would not forgive him. He had stolen something from their lives."

Despite the crushing loss, Louis kept fighting. Joe's career came to an end for good in October 1951 when he faced Rocky Marciano, a hard-punching, up-and-coming heavyweight. The battering Louis got that night convinced him that he was finished as a fighter. Marciano went on to win the heavyweight title and became the only champion to go undefeated.

Joe retired with a record 68 victories. He lost only three times. He held the championship for 11 years, 8 months—a record that still stands.

Joe's final years were not pretty. To pay his taxes, Joe refereed boxing matches and went on tour as a professional wrestler. Another marriage failed, and then he married a third time. He had problems with drugs and alcohol. During the 1970s, he took a job as a greeter at a Las Vegas casino. In the afternoons, he played golf. Evenings he was in the casino, earning a paycheck by welcoming tourists.

In October 1977, Louis suffered a serious heart attack. He managed to survive, but afterward he lived his life from a wheelchair.

On April 11, 1981, Louis attended a championship fight at the sports pavilion of a Las Vegas hotel. A friend wheeled Joe down the aisle toward a space that had been reserved for him. As he rolled along, fans spotted him and clapped and shouted greetings. Then the entire crowd stood and applauded and cheered. It was Joe Louis's last standing ovation. The next morning he suffered another major heart attack and died.

AFTERWORD

The memory of Joe Louis has faded now. By the time the American civil rights movement gained force in the mid-1950s, a good number of other African Americans were being hailed as national heroes. Jackie Robinson was playing baseball for the Brooklyn Dodgers. In the National Football League, Jim Brown was setting records that would last for decades. Bill Russell was on his way to a Hall of Fame career with the NBA's Boston Celtics. In Montgomery, Alabama, Rosa Parks refused to give up her seat on a public bus to a white passenger. Her courageous act triggered the Montgomery bus boycott, headed by Dr. Martin Luther King, Jr. In the years afterward, mass mobilization and other acts of nonviolent civil disobedience, plus lawsuits and lobbying efforts, eventually led to the passage of laws forbidding discrimination on the basis of race, religion, age, or sex.

Joe Louis listened and watched Dr. King through the years. "He was the new champion," Louis said. He admired Dr. King, he said, because he "showed black people they could make things change by working together."

As for his own contribution, Joe said this: "I had tried in my way to ease the load as far as race relations go, but I was out there just by myself." Joe took no credit for the important role he played as an American hero, reigning as a source of pride and inspiration for American blacks for decades. Joe Louis "proved we were the strongest people in the world," said Maya Angelou in her book *I Know Why the Caged Bird Sings*.

Joe Louis did more. He offered a challenge to the conscience of a country. Through much of his life, the thoughts and feelings of a majority of Americans were not reflected by the nation's actions.

In recognition of Louis and all that he achieved, his son and boxing greats gathered at Louis's gravesite at Arlington National Cemetery in 1986 on the 72nd anniversary of his birth. The group included (left to right): Michael Spinks, heavyweight champion at the time; former heavyweight champions Jersey Joe Walcott, Joe Frazier, and Muhammad Ali; former welterweight champion Sugar Ray Leonard; and Joseph Louis Barrow, Jr.

"You couldn't have it both ways," Louis's son, Joe Louis Barrow, Jr., has pointed out. "You couldn't put Joe Louis on a pedestal and admire him as the heavyweight champion of the world and not allow him and his people to eat where they wanted to eat, live where they wanted to live, and be educated where they wanted to be educated."

When Joe Louis died, President Ronald Reagan praised him for his patriotism. At the request of Louis's widow, the president made it possible for Louis to be buried at Arlington National Cemetery. That was fitting. Arlington is the final resting place for American heroes.

CHRONOLOGY

A felt pennant sold by vendors at the Joe Louis-Billy Conn fight in 1941.

May 13, 1914
Joe Louis Barrow is born in Chambers County, Alabama.

1926
The Brooks-Barrow family moves to Detroit.

1932
Louis begins boxing training in a Detroit gym and enters competition as an amateur.

July 4, 1934
A Golden Gloves champion as an amateur, Louis becomes a professional and scores a knockout in his first pro fight.

June 25, 1935
Louis defeats Primo Carnera, the first of several former heavyweight champions he is to beat.

June 19, 1936
After 27 consecutive victories as a professional, Louis suffers his first defeat, losing to Max Schmeling.

June 22, 1937
Louis defeats James J. Braddock to win the heavyweight championship.

June 22, 1938
In a rematch, Louis knocks out Max Schmeling in the first round.

January 9, 1942
Louis defeats Max Baer by knocking him out in the eighth round. With the United States engulfed in World War II, Louis donates his prize money to the Navy Relief Society.

January 10, 1942
Louis enlists in the U.S. Army.

March 27, 1942
Louis defeats Abe Simon and donates his earnings to the Army Relief Fund.

October 1, 1945
After almost four years of service, Louis is discharged from the Army.

June 19, 1946
In his first bout after returning to civilian life, Louis defeats Billy Conn.

March 1, 1949
Louis retires as heavyweight champion.

September 27, 1950
Louis returns to the ring and loses to heavyweight champion Ezzard Charles.

October 26, 1951
Louis is knocked out in the eighth round by Rocky Marciano, who goes on to capture the heavyweight championship. Louis retires a second time, never to fight again.

April 12, 1981
Louis dies of a heart attack in Las Vegas, Nevada.

1993
The U.S. Postal Service issues a postage stamp honoring Louis.

2003
Ring Magazine ranks Louis No. 1 on its list of the 100 greatest punchers of all time.

2005
The International Boxing Research Association singles out Louis as the greatest heavyweight of all time.

RESOURCES

BOOKS

Astor, Gerald. *". . . And a Credit to His Race."* New York: E. P. Dutton, 1974.

Barrow, Jr., Joe Louis with Barbara Munder. *Joe Louis: 50 Years an American Hero.* New York: McGraw-Hill, 1988.

Campbell, Jim. *The Importance of Joe Louis.* San Diego: Lucent Books, 1997.

Jakoubek, Robert. *Joe Louis: Heavyweight Champion.* New York: Chelsea House, 1990.

Lipsyte, Robert. *Joe Louis: A Champ for All America.* New York: HarperCollins, 1994.

Louis, Joe with Edna and Art Rust, Jr. *Joe Louis: My Life.* New York: Harcourt Brace Jovanovich, 1978.

Margolick, David. *Beyond Glory: Joe Louis vs. Max Schmeling and a World on the Brink.* New York: Alfred A. Knopf, 2005.

MAGAZINES

"High Tide in Harlem, Joe Louis as a Symbol of Freedom," *New Masses*, July 1938, pp. 18–20.

VIDEOS

Joe Louis—For All Time, MPI Home Video, 1994

The Joe Louis Story, Entertainment Programs, Inc., 1953

DVD

The Joe Louis Story, Ellstree Hill Entertainment, 1953

QUOTATION SOURCES

Quotations that appear in this book have been taken from the sources listed here, most of which are cited in full on page 62.

Page 5 "All my life my hands felt important to me. . . ." *Joe Louis vs. Max Schmeling and a World on the Brink*, David Margolick, p. 60, from "In This Corner. . . . Joe Louis," produced and written by Mel Baily, directed by Arthur Forest, WNEW-TV, July 21, 1963, in Museum of Television and Radio, New York

Page 10 "Momma was a big woman. . . ." Joe Louis with Edna and Art Rust, Jr., p. 3

Page 11 "She worked as hard . . ." *Joe Louis: My Life*, Joe Louis with Edna and Art Rust, Jr., p. 4

Page 13 "He was always fair. . . ." Joe Louis with Edna and Art Rust, Jr., p. 8

Page 13 (caption) ". . . too much for me," Joe Louis with Edna and Art Rust, Jr., p. 14

Pages 16–17 "When I quit school . . ." Joe Louis with Edna and Art Rust, Jr., p. 23

Page 19 "That's OK . . ." *Joe Louis: Heavyweight Champion*, Robert Jakoubek, p. 19

Page 19 "These were really tough guys. . . ." Joe Louis with Edna and Art Rust, Jr., p. 28

Page 21 "I think you're ready. . . ." Joe Louis with Edna and Art Rust, Jr., p. 31

Page 22 "OK, I'm ready. . . ." Joe Louis with Edna and Art Rust, Jr., p. 33

Page 22 "I would have gone anyway. . . ." Joe Louis with Edna and Art Rust, Jr., p. 33

Page 23 "The white man . . ." Jakoubek, p. 48

Page 24 "If you're black and at the top . . ." Joe Louis with Edna and Art Rust, Jr., p. 125

Page 25 "Don't be another . . ." Jakoubek, p. 52

Page 25 "To be a champion . . ." Jakoubek, p. 52

Page 26 "Classy looking," Joe Louis with Edna and Art Rust, Jr., p. 45

Page 27 "It was love at first sight," Jakoubek, p. 66

Page 27 "You're our savior, Joe!" Joe Louis with Edna and Art Rust, Jr., pp. 48, 49

Pages 28–29 "Mail was coming in by the ton. . . ." Joe Louis with Edna and Art Rust, Jr., p. 67

Page 30: "Mike Jacobs's pet pickaninny," Margolick, p. 133

Page 30: "Joseph, make me up a sentence. . . ." Margolick, p. 133

Page 33: "I jes' kept on hittin' him. . . ." *The Washington Post*, June 26, 1935

Pages 34–35 "I've always considered the Baer fight . . ." Joe Louis with Edna and Art Rust, Jr., p. 73

Page 37 "I guarantee you . . ." Margolick, p. 130

Page 37 "too sure of himself . . ." Margolick, p. 371, from *Boston Globe*, June 17, 1936.

Page 38 "For God's sake . . ." Jakoubek, p. 72

Page 39 "a whole race of people" Joe Louis with Edna and Art Rust, Jr. p.90

Page 40 "Joe's mad at Schmeling. . . ." Jakoubek, p. 74

Page 41 "The one-time cotton picker . . ." Joe Louis with Edna and Art Rust, Jr., p. 118

Page 42 "A new world's champion . . ." Margolick, p. 229

Page 42 "We want Schmeling!" Margolick, p. 230

Page 43 "Joe, we're depending on those muscles. . . ." Joe Louis with Edna and Art Rust, Jr. p. 137

Page 43 "Let me tell you, that was a thrill . . . ." Joe Louis with Edna and Art Rust, Jr., p. 137

Page 43 "I don't like Schmeling. . . ." Margolick, p. 265

Page 45 "How do you feel, Joe? . . ." Joe Louis with Edna and Art Rust, Jr., p. 141

Page 45 "rarin' to go"

Page 45 "They're ready . . ." Margolick, p. 45

Page 46 "Move, Max, move!" Jakoubek, p. 23

Page 46 "A right to the body . . ." Margolick, p. 300

Page 46 "The fight is over. . . ." Margolick, p. 301

Page 46 "They shouted, sang, laughed . . ." "High Tide in Harlem, Joe Louis as a Symbol of Freedom," *New Masses*, July 5, 1939, pp. 18-20

Page 46 "Joe knocked out Hitler cold!" Margolick, p. 316

Page 46 "Boy, am I glad . . ." Margolick, p. 317

Page 47 "I had the championship . . ." Joe Louis with Edna and Art Rust, Jr., p. 144

Pages 48–49 "He never hurt me. . . ." Margolick, p. 308, from *Pittsburgh Courier*, June 25, 1938

Page 50 "When I was being discharged . . ." Joe Louis with Edna and Art Rust, Jr., p. 190

Page 51 "I'm not going to box" Jakoubek, p. 101

Page 54 "My crazy little world was crumbling. . . ." Joe Louis with Edna and Art Rust, Jr., pp. 217, 218

Page 55 "They should have called him. . . ." Margolick, p. 344

Pages 56–57 "The papers and magazines had all kinds of articles. . . ." Joe Louis with Edna and Art Rust, Jr., pp. 232, 233

Page 58 "It didn't matter. . . ." Jakoubek, p. 114

Page 60 "He was the new champion. . . ." Joe Louis with Edna and Art Rust, Jr., p. 245

Page 60 "I had tried . . ." Joe Louis with Edna and Art Rust, Jr., p. 245

Page 61 "You couldn't have it both ways. . . ." *The Detroit Free Press*, August 13, 2006

Jacket back "If you're black and at the top . . ." Joe Louis with Edna and Art Rust, Jr., p. 125

The U.S. Treasury issued this coin in 1981 in Louis's honor.

INDEX

Founded in 1888, the National Geographic Society is one of the largest nonprofit scientific and educational organizations in the world. It reaches more than 285 million people worldwide each month through its official journal, NATIONAL GEOGRAPHIC, and its four other magazines; the National Geographic Channel; television documentaries; radio programs; films; books; videos and DVDs; maps; and interactive media. National Geographic has funded more than 8,000 scientific research projects and supports an education program combating geographic illiteracy.

For more information, please call 1-800-NGS LINE (647-5463) or write to the following address:
National Geographic Society
1145 17th Street N.W., Washington, D.C. 20036-4688 U.S.A.

Visit us online at www.nationalgeographic.com/books

For librarians and teachers:
www.ngchildrensbooks.com

More for kids from National Geographic:
kids.nationalgeographic.com

For information about special discounts for bulk purchases, please contact National Geographic Books Special Sales: ngspecsales@ngs.org

For rights or permissions inquiries, please contact National Geographic Books Subsidiary Rights: ngbookrights@ngs.org